D1123959

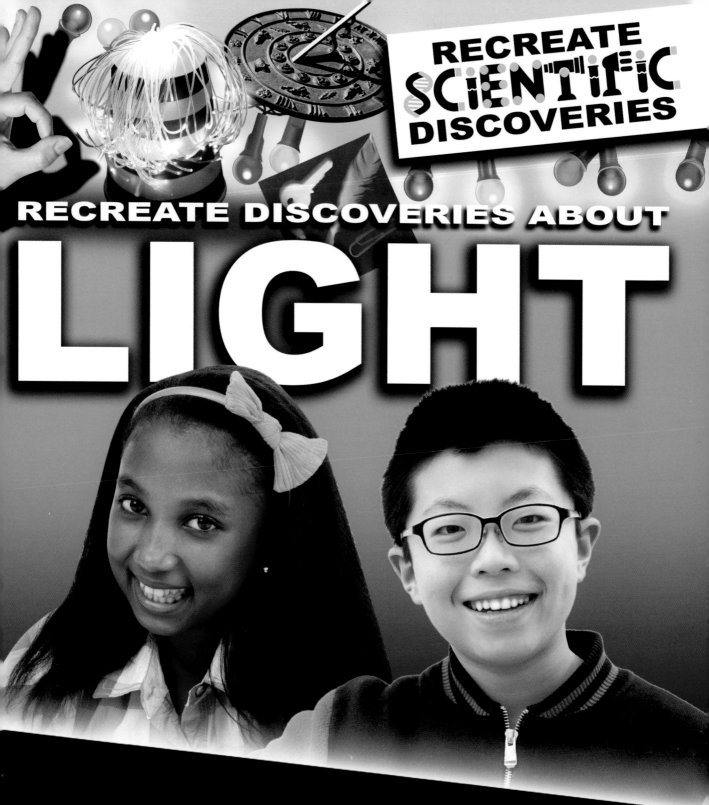

RECREATE SCIENTIFIC DISCOVERIES

RECREATE DISCOVERIES ABOUT
LIGHT

CRABTREE
PUBLISHING COMPANY
WWW.CRABTREEBOOKS.COM

ANNA CLAYBOURNE

RECREATE SCiENTiFiC DISCOVERIES

Author:
Anna Claybourne

Editorial director:
Kathy Middleton

Editors:
Sarah Silver
Sheri Doyle

Proofreader:
Heather Hewer

Interior design:
Eoin Norton & Katherine Berti

Cover design:
Katherine Berti

Photo research:
Diana Morris

Print and production coordinator:
Katherine Berti

Images:
All images by Eoin Norton for Wayland except the following:
Alamy: Science History Images: p. 12tr, 16tr
Dreamstime: Sherpa03: p. 22tl
Getty Images
    Caitlind r.c. Brown & Wayne Garrett. Photo Mica Radek/AFP: p. 5b
iStockphoto
    Antagain: p. 25b
    Nikada: p. 29t
Jeff Wall: Courtesy of the artist: p. 24tr, 24cl
    (1993, transparency in lightbox, 229.0 x 377.0)
J.L. Lovell, University of Massachusetts Amherst: p. 10tr
Kumi Yamashita: Courtesy of the artist: p. 6cl, 6tr
NGA Washington: p. 18cl
Shutterstock: front cover (sundial, light bulbs, hand, stationery), p. 4cl, 13 cr
    Aleks49: p. 22tr
    Alex Hubanov: p. 23br
    Everett Historical: p. 5tl
    Kevin Lavorgna: p. 5tr
    maxpro: p. 4tr
    Oliver Hoffmann: p. 14br
    pixelklex: p. 21bl
    vladee: p. 29b
Tracey Emin: Courtesy of the artist: p. 26tr
    Courtesy of Lehmann Maupin, © Tracey Emin.
      All rights reserved, DACS/Artimage 2017: p. 26b
Vicki DaSilva Visual Artist, vickidasilva.com, lightgraffiti.com: p. 20tr, 20b
Wikimedia Commons
    de Larmessin: p. 8tr
    Jeroen Rouwema: p. 12br
    PD: p. 18tr
    Wellcome Library: p. 12bl
Every attempt has been made to clear copyright. Should there be any inadvertent omission please apply to the publisher for rectification.

Library and Archives Canada Cataloguing in Publication

Claybourne, Anna, author
    Recreate discoveries about light / Anna Claybourne.

(Recreate scientific discoveries)
Includes index.
Issued in print and electronic formats.
ISBN 978-0-7787-5052-9 (hardcover).--
ISBN 978-0-7787-5065-9 (softcover).--
ISBN 978-1-4271-2151-6 (HTML)

    1. Light--Experiments--Juvenile literature. I. Title.

QC365.C53 2018   j535.078   C2018-902451-8
                           C2018-902452-6

Library of Congress Cataloging-in-Publication Data

Names: Claybourne, Anna, author.
Title: Recreate discoveries about light / Anna Claybourne.
Description: New York, New York : Crabtree Publishing, [2019] |
    Series: Recreate scientific discoveries | Includes index.
Identifiers: LCCN 2018021344 (print) | LCCN 2018025017 (ebook) |
    ISBN 9781427121516 (Electronic) |
    ISBN 9780778750529 (hardcover) |
    ISBN 9780778750659 (pbk.)
Subjects: LCSH: Light--Experiments--Juvenile literature. |
    Science--Experiments--Juvenile literature.
Classification: LCC QC365 (ebook) | LCC QC365 .C6225 2019 (print) |
    DDC 535.078--dc23
LC record available at https://lccn.loc.gov/2018021344

Crabtree Publishing Company

www.crabtreebooks.com   1-800-387-7650

Published in 2019 by Crabtree Publishing Company

Published in Canada
Crabtree Publishing
616 Welland Ave.
St. Catharines, Ontario
L2M 5V6

Published in the United States
Crabtree Publishing
PMB 59051
350 Fifth Avenue, 59th Floor
New York, New York 10118

Note:

In preparation of this book, all due care has been exercised with regard to the instructions, activities and techniques depicted. The publishers regret that they can accept no liability for any loss or injury sustained. Always follow the manufacturers' advice when using electric and battery-powered appliances.

The website addresses (URLs) included in this book were valid at the time of going to press. It is possible that some addresses may have changed or sites may have changed or closed down since publication. While the author and publishers regret any inconvenience this may cause to the readers, no responsibility for any such changes can be accepted by either the author or the publishers.

Printed in the U.S.A./082018/CG20180601

CONTENTS

TAKE CARE!

You can make these projects with materials and tools found at home, or in a grocery store, craft store, or hardware store. Some of the projects involve the use of sharp or breakable objects, or need extra strength to operate. Please get permission to do these projects, and make sure an adult is available to help

UNDERSTANDING LIGHT

Light is important for all of us. The sun gives us daylight and warmth, and it helps plants grow, providing food for animals and humans. We use **artificial** lights to help us do things at night. And we use light in many machines, such as tablets, cameras, movie projectors, laser printers, and **solar-powered** cars.

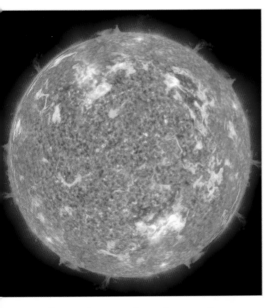

The sun is a star that releases a huge amount of light energy. Without it, most life on Earth could not exist.

WHAT IS LIGHT?

Light is a form of energy that travels at a very high speed and can move across empty space. It is made up of energy waves and has a range of different **wavelengths**. Different colors of light have different wavelengths.

Light energy has a wide spectrum of wavelengths, from very long to very short.

*Long wavelength light includes **radio waves** and **microwaves**.*

*Most wavelengths are invisible to us. The only light we can see, called **visible light**, is the medium wavelength light in the middle (below).*

*Short wavelength light includes **x-rays**.*

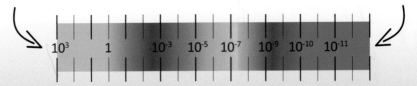

10^3 1 10^{-3} 10^{-5} 10^{-7} 10^{-9} 10^{-10} 10^{-11}

Visible light ranges from longer-wavelength red light to shorter-wavelength violet light.

LIGHT INVENTIONS

People have been using light to make and invent things for a very long time. A prehistoric monument, called Stonehenge (right), was built to line up with the sunrise at particular times of year, working as an early version of a calendar. Mirrors, shadow clocks, and lamps have existed since ancient times. Some of the most important inventions in history have made use of light, including the light bulb, cameras, microscopes, telescopes, **fiber optics**, and solar power.

American inventor Thomas Edison (1847–1931) is often credited as the inventor the light bulb, but many different inventors contributed to the idea.

ART AND LIGHT

Light has always been important for visual artists. Painters, such as Caravaggio (1571–1610), used light and shade to create lifelike masterpieces. Artists today use film, electric light, and photography to make changing, interactive works of art.

A sculpture titled Cloud was on display in Brno in the Czech Republic in 2014. It's made of hundreds of light bulbs and was created by Canadian artists Caitlind r.c. Brown and Wayne Garrett.

ART IN SHADOWS

SHADOWS

Create your own artworks by playing around with light and shadow.

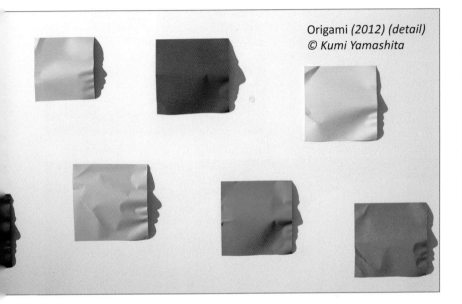

Origami *(2012) (detail)*
© *Kumi Yamashita*

"I sculpt using light and shadow. I construct single or multiple objects and place them in relation to a single light source. The complete artwork is therefore composed of both the material (the solid objects) and the immaterial (the light or shadow)."

– *Kumi Yamashita*

KUMI YAMASHITA

(1968–)

New York-based Japanese artist Kumi Yamashita creates light and shadow sculptures from everyday objects.

At first glance, her work may appear to be the silhouettes of people, but look closely and they are actually sheets of paper attached to walls. She also uses an assortment of wood blocks, fabrics, and steel plates to create the sculptures.

She shines light on these at just the right angle, which transforms them into extraordinary works of art.

WHAT YOU NEED

- aluminum foil
- scissors
- masking tape
- flashlight
- a wall to display your art on

1

Step 1

Cut out or fold a sheet of aluminum foil into a rectangle, no smaller than 12 inches x 8 inches (30 cm x 20 cm).

2

Step 2

Use one edge of the foil to shape the portrait. Create shapes along the edge that will form the outline of your portrait. Do this by pinching and sculpting the foil to form parts that stick out for the forehead, nose, lips, and chin.

3

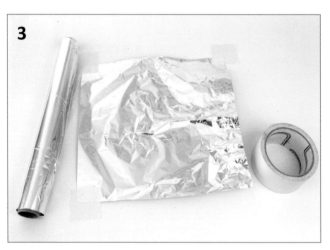

Step 3

Use a piece of masking tape on the corners of the foil sheet to attach it to the wall.

4

Step 4

Turn the lights off and shine the flashlight towards your foil sheet. Move the flashlight around until you get the shadow you like.

CASTING SHADOWS

Shadows are made when an object blocks light. Light travels in straight lines, so it can't curve around the object. Instead, it leaves a dark area in the shape of the object. The shape of a shadow can be stretched, depending on the angle the light is coming from. Shining the light from the side makes the small shapes in the edge of the foil cast longer shadows.

SUNDOWN SHADOWS

The same thing happens with your own shadow. At midday, when the sun is high overhead, your shadow is short. In the evening, when the sun is lower near the horizon, your shadow is much longer.

A NEW VIEW

See around corners or over walls with this old but fascinating invention.

WHAT YOU NEED

- two small mirrors, available from craft stores
- a long, rectangular cardboard box that's slightly wider than your mirrors (such as a fruit juice carton)
- adhesive putty
- scissors
- a marker
- a protractor
- piece of paper
- tape

JOHANNES GUTENBERG

(c. 1398–1468)

German inventor Johannes Gutenberg lived in the 1400s. He is most famous for developing the printing press in about 1440. In the 1430s, he's thought to have made the first **periscopes** to help people to see over the crowds at religious shrines and festivals!

1

Step 1

To make the periscope, you'll need to cut open one of the wider sides of the box. If necessary, tape any other openings closed.

2

Step 2

Draw two squares on the narrower sides of the box, one at one end, and one at the other end on the opposite side. Cut them out.

3

Step 3

Use a protractor to fold a corner of your paper at a 45° angle. Cut the corner off, and put it in the corner inside one end of the box, making sure the sloping angle faces one of the holes. Draw along the edge to mark the angle for the mirror. Turn the box around, and do the same at the other end.

4

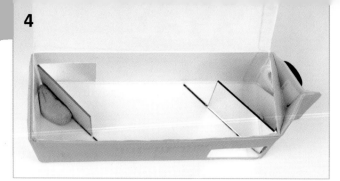

Step 4

Roll two large lumps of adhesive putty, and stick them to the backs of the two mirrors. Press the mirrors into place in each of the ends of the box, so that their reflecting surfaces line up with the lines you have drawn.

5

Step 5

Close the side of the box and check your periscope by looking into the hole at the bottom end. You might need to adjust the mirrors a little. You should be able to look into one end and see out of the other!

6

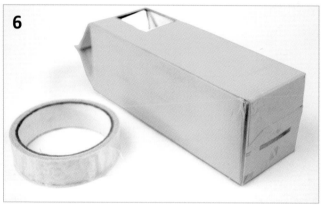

Step 6

Once you're sure your periscope works, use tape to close the open side of the box. You can also paint or decorate it.

SEEING AROUND A CORNER

A periscope lets you see around a corner, over a wall, or over a crowd by changing the direction of **light rays**. It works because of the **reflection** that happens when light bounces off mirrors at the same angle as it hits the mirror.

Light ray hits at a 45° angle

Light ray reflects off at a 45° angle

Light ray turns 90°, or a right angle

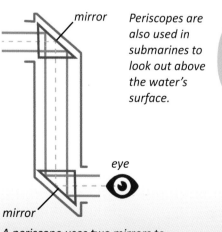

mirror

Periscopes are also used in submarines to look out above the water's surface.

eye

mirror

A periscope uses two mirrors to collect light at one end of the box, and bounce it out at the other. When it reaches your eyes, they see the view from the other end of the box.

CURVED LIGHT

Honor the inventor of fiber optic tubes with your own homemade fiber optic lamp.

"Be it known that I, WILLIAM WHEELER... have invented a new and useful Improvement in Apparatus for Lighting Dwellings."
– *William Wheeler*

WILLIAM WHEELER

(1851–1932)

William Wheeler was an American engineer and teacher who used pipes to build water supply systems. In 1880, he tried using pipes to carry light instead. He designed a set of linked glass tubes with a reflective coating. Light could be shone into one end, then carried along the pipes and around corners to any room in a house, using reflection. This was one of the first steps towards the invention of modern **fiber optic cables**.

WHAT YOU NEED

- at least 10 feet (3 m) of clear, stretchy beading cord, more if you like, up to about 33 feet (10 m)
- a piece of cardboard
- paper cup
- scissors
- tape
- adhesive putty
- a bright mini LED flashlight, shorter than your paper cup
- aluminum foil

Step 1

Have a piece of tape ready, about 4 inches (10 cm) long. Wind about 10–33 feet (3–10 m) of beading cord around a piece of cardboard.

Step 2

Remove the bundle of cord from the cardboard and wind the piece of tape around one end of it.

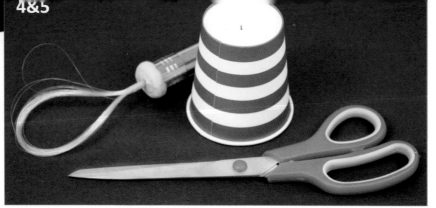

Step 3

Cut off the shorter end of the bundle neatly, so that the ends of the cord bundle are all lined up together and held in place by the tape.

Step 4

Roll a small amount of adhesive putty tightly around the taped end of the cord bundle and then push this firmly onto the end of your flashlight so that no light shows through.

Step 5

Use the scissors to make a hole in the bottom of the cup, as wide as your bundle of cord.

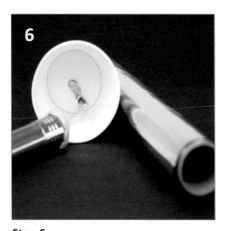

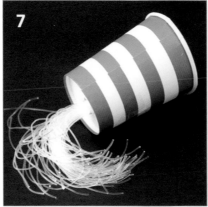

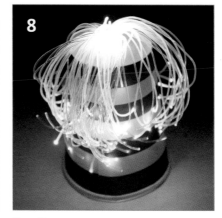

Step 6

Fold the bundle of cord and put some foil over the top end (this makes it easier to thread them). Thread the bundle through the hole in the cup, from the inside.

Step 7

Gently push the flashlight up inside the cup, and remove the foil from the the cord. Cut through the loop with scissors so that the cords spray out in all directions.

Step 8

Switch on the flashlight and take your fiber optic lamp to a dark room. The light should travel to the ends of the cords, appearing as shining dots.

INTERNAL REFLECTION

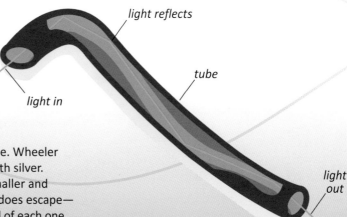

Wheeler's lighting tubes and your fiber optic lamp both work using **internal reflection**—light moving through a curving tube by reflecting back and forth.

It only works if light can bounce off the inside of the tube. Wheeler made his glass tubes extra reflective by coating them with silver. Modern glass fiber optic cables are similar, but much smaller and very flexible. With the beading cords, a little bit of light does escape— but enough is reflected to carry a point of light to the end of each one.

A CLOSER LOOK

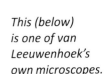

Make a microscope, and discover a hidden world like scientist Antonie van Leeuwenhoek did!

> "I then most always saw, with great wonder, that in the said matter there were many very little living animalcules, very prettily a-moving.
> – *Antonie van Leeuwenhoek*

ANTONIE VAN LEEUWENHOEK

(1632–1723)

Dutch shopkeeper and scientist Antonie van Leeuwenhoek sold cloth and used magnifying glasses to inspect fabrics. By heating and melting glass, he managed to make tiny glass spheres that worked as very powerful magnifiers. He mounted each sphere in a metal plate, making the first microscopes. He soon realized there was a lot more to look at close up than just cloth. In fact, his invention led him to discover **microbes**—tiny living things such as **bacteria**. He called them **animalcules**.

This (below) is one of van Leeuwenhoek's own microscopes.

William Heath's cartoon Monster Soup, *c. 1928, shows a woman looking through a microscope to discover the supposed impurity of the River Thames in London.*

WHAT YOU NEED

- a piece of card stock
- a clear plastic craft sheet
- scissors
- tape
- a large, sharp needle
- a wooden skewer
- petroleum jelly
- a small bowl and some water
- two paper cups or cans
- a small glass
- objects to look at, such as feathers, leaves, or flowers

YUCK!

People were astonished to discover this new world of tiny creepy-crawly life all around them. For scientists, it led to many important new discoveries, such as how germs cause infections and diseases, and how to fight them.

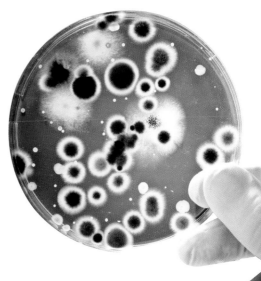

Step 1

Cut a rectangular hole in the middle of your card. Cut a piece of the clear plastic craft sheet in a rectangular shape slightly larger than the hole in the card stock.

Step 2

Place the cut plastic over the hole, and stick the edges in place with Scotch tape. Use the needle to carefully make a hole in the middle of the plastic.

Step 3

Smear some petroleum jelly onto the pointed end of the wooden skewer. Push the skewer through the hole. This will make the hole bigger and add an oily barrier around it.

Step 4

Stand the card on the two cups or cans so that the hole is in the middle with nothing underneath it. Fill the bowl with water and dip the skewer into it.

Step 5

Carefully drip drops of water into the tiny hole.

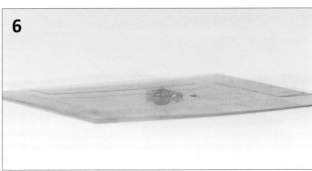

Step 6

You should see a drop of water sitting in the hole. If it doesn't work or you spill water, gently clean it off with paper towels and try again.

Step 7

To use the microscope, turn your glass upside down and put your object (such as a leaf) on top of it. Slide it carefully under the water drop.

The drop of water works like the tiny round glass sphere in van Leeuwenhoek's version.

8

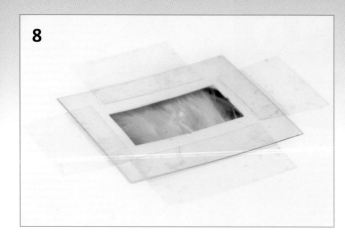

Step 8

Shut one eye and use the other to look as closely as you can at the water drop. Press down gently on the card to get it at just the right distance, and you should see your object magnified.

LENSES AND LIGHT

The round water drop works as a **lens**—a curved, clear object that bends light by **refraction**. As light passes between the air and the water, the change in material makes the light rays bend, or refract. When the bent light reaches your eye, it makes the object you are looking at appear much bigger, and you can see tiny details.

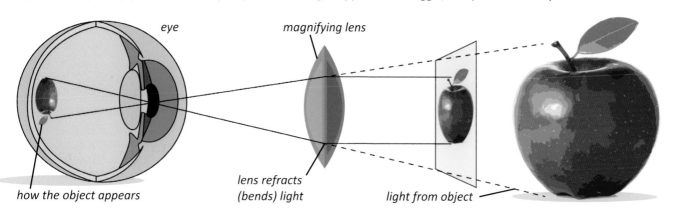

eye   *magnifying lens*

how the object appears

lens refracts (bends) light

light from object

A normal magnifying glass works the same way, but its lens is flatter and less powerful. Van Leeuwenhoek found that a very small sphere makes light refract much more. A water drop isn't a perfect sphere, but it's almost as good (and easier to make!).

TRY THIS!

If you have a smartphone, you may be able to line up the camera lens on the phone with the water drop, allowing you to see the images more clearly and take photos of them.

There's another method too—but only try this if you have permission (and only with an old phone). Also, only do this with a lens that's covered in glass and not close to the phone's microphone. Hold the phone with its camera facing up, and use your finger to drip a small water drop directly over the middle of the lens.

Carefully turn the phone over with a semicircular movement, so that the drop stays in place. You can then use the phone's camera as a microscope to look at and photograph things in close-up! (It may take a few attempts to get it right.)

MAKE THE WORLD UPSIDE DOWN

Build your own viewer to see the world upside down like an inventive scientist did centuries ago!

WHAT YOU NEED

- empty cylindrical potato chip tube
- tracing paper
- pencil or marker
- ruler
- sharp knife
- scissors
- thumbtack
- strong Scotch tape
- aluminum foil

IBN AL-HAYTHAM

(965–1040)

This pioneering scientist made key discoveries about the nature of sight.

He was the first person to prove, through experiments, that light travels in straight lines and bounces off objects. To aid his investigations, he invented a chamber known as a **camera obscura**. It was a dark room, with a tiny opening to let in light. Ibn al-Haytham found that this captured an image of the world outside, which appeared upside-down on the opposite wall. This also helped him prove that vision occurs when light enters the eye, rather than from the eye emitting light as was commonly believed.

1

Step 1

Take the plastic lid off the cylindrical potato chip tube, but don't throw it away. Draw a line with the pencil all the way around the tube, about 2 inches (5 cm) up from the bottom.

Step 2

Ask an adult to use the knife to cut along the line so the tube is in two pieces.

2

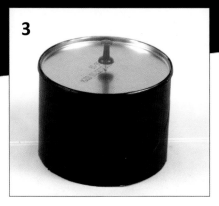

3

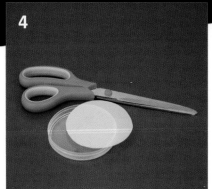

4

Step 3

The shorter piece has a metal end. With an adult's help, make a hole in the center of the metal with a thumbtack.

Step 4

Cut out a piece of tracing paper that fits just inside the lid of the potato chip tube, and place it inside the lid. It should fit tightly so it doesn't fall out when tipped up. This will act as a screen.

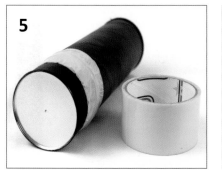

5

6

Step 5

Put the lid on the top of the shorter piece of the tube. Join the two pieces of tube together using Scotch tape.

Step 6

Tape one end of the aluminum foil to the tube. Wrap the foil all the way round the tube twice, and tape down the end. This will keep light out of the tube.

7

Step 7

The viewer will work best on a bright, sunny day. Go outside, or stand near a bright window. Close one eye and hold the tube up to your other eye. The inside of the tube should be as dark as possible, so cup your hands around the opening of the tube if you need to.

> As you look through the tube, you'll see the world upside down!

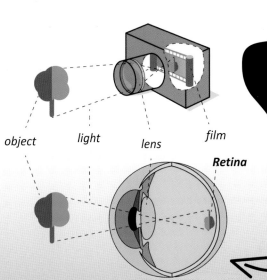

object *light* *lens* *film*

Retina

YOUR EYE AS A CAMERA

Your viewer is a type of camera obscura, like al-Haytham's dark room. When light rays pass through the pinhole, they cross over to the opposite side. This creates an upside-down image of the outside world on the screen. Cameras and the human eye work in the same way.

SUN PRINTS

Use the Sun to capture images of everyday and natural objects, like photography pioneer Thomas Wedgwood.

There are two ways of making sun prints, depending on which type of paper you have. You could try both and compare them.

THOMAS WEDGWOOD

(1771–1805)

Thomas Wedgwood came from a famous family of pottery makers. He had deep interests in art and scientific experiments. He was especially interested in light and images. In the 1790s, Wedgwood found a way to capture an image of an object, such as a piece of lace or a leaf. He put an object on paper or on leather coated with silver nitrate, a light-sensitive chemical, and left them in the sun. Where the sunlight reached the paper, it changed it to a darker color. Where the sunlight was blocked by the object, a lighter image remained.

Wedgwood called the images "sun prints" or "sun pictures." They were a type of early photographs. But Wedgwood couldn't find a way to preserve or keep the images—daylight would eventually turn the paper black all over. The prints could only be preserved by keeping them in the dark. It would be many more years before permanent photos were invented.

WHAT YOU NEED

- everyday objects that are mostly flat, such as flowers, leaves, keys, string, coins, buttons, and beads
- a sunny windowsill or any other safe, sunny spot
- dark-colored sugar paper or construction paper, or specially made sun print paper from an art supply or craft store
- a tray and a container of water (if using sun print paper)

THE CONSTRUCTION PAPER METHOD

Step 1

Spread out a sheet of construction paper in your sunny spot. It needs to be in a place where it won't get moved or disturbed by the wind, pets, or people.

Step 2

Arrange a selection of objects on the paper to make a pattern, design, or picture. Then leave the paper in the sun for as long as you can—all day, if possible.

Step 3

Remove the objects and look at your print. Sunlight fades the paper, making it paler. Where the objects were, you'll see a darker image.

THE SUN PRINT PAPER METHOD:

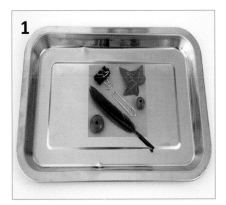

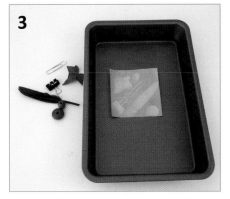

Step 1

Sun print paper is much more light-sensitive, so you have to work faster. Remove one piece of paper from the pack (and seal the pack tightly). Put the paper on the tray, blue side up, and arrange your objects on it.

Step 2

Move the tray into the sunlight and wait until the paper around the objects has turned white or very pale blue. In bright sunlight, this should only take two minutes. If it's less sunny, it could take up to half an hour.

Step 3

Move the tray out of the sun. Quickly remove the objects and put the paper into the water. Leave it there for at least a minute to develop, then take it out and leave it to dry. You will now have a preserved pale image on a darker background.

COLOR CHANGES

There are several substances that are sensitive to bright light. Sunlight breaks down the ink in the construction paper, making it fade. You might have noticed that colors fade on curtains or a poster that's been in the sun for a long time.

Sun print paper is coated with chemicals that react to light. When the paper is soaked in water, the areas exposed to the light become darker, creating a clear image of the objects.

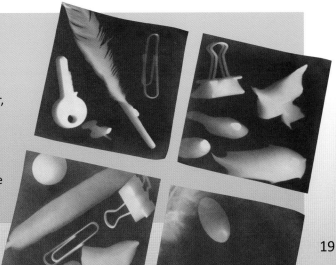

PAINTING WITH LIGHT

Make your own "light graffiti" like pioneering artist Vicki DaSilva.

" This light graffiti...this legal graffiti... this medium where I can go anywhere, and write anything. "
– Vicki DaSilva

VICKI DASILVA

(1960–)

American artist Vicki DaSilva paints with light and creates works of art she calls "light graffiti." Wearing a dark outfit, she moves large fluorescent lamps around to make patterns, pictures, or messages in rooms or on buildings, landscapes, and famous landmarks. She photographs the light paintings using a camera with a long exposure. She's made light paintings in all kinds of places, such as beaches, art galleries, and city streets. She's even made light paintings on the Eiffel Tower and the White House.

WHAT YOU NEED

- a smartphone or tablet with a camera
- an app that allows you to take long exposures, such as Slow Shutter Cam, NightCap or LongExpo (always ask an adult about buying an app)
- light sources, such as glow sticks, toys with flashing lights, or a small flashlight
- a smartphone tripod, if possible

Vicki DaSilva slows down and speeds up her light source to give texture to her works, as in this light painting, East River Esplanade #3, *2014.*

1

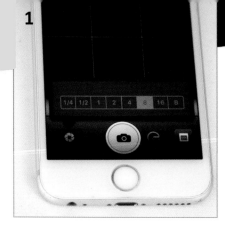

2

Step 1

Download your app and try out the settings to set the exposure time. An exposure time of about 10 seconds is a good place to start.

Step 2

Set up your phone or tablet somewhere dark— it could be a room with the lights off, or a dark yard. If possible, use a tripod to hold it still. If you don't have a tripod, ask someone to operate the phone or tablet while resting it on a table or stable surface.

3

4

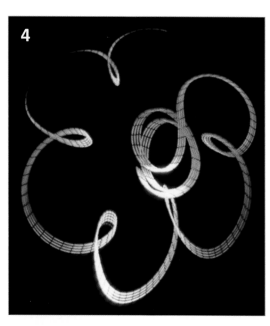

Step 3

Get your light sources ready, and stand in view of the camera. Start the long exposure shot, and while it is running, use the light sources to draw shapes, patterns, or words in the air.

Step 4

When the shot is finished, check out your picture. You should be able to see an image made up of the lines of light you have drawn. Experiment with different camera settings, light sources, and styles. Save and print the pictures you like most.

You can "paint" words, objects, and abstract shapes.

LIGHT TRAILS

A digital camera is sensitive to light. For a normal photo, the camera records light only for a split second, to give a sharp image of a single moment. A longer exposure, lasting several seconds, collects all the light that enters the camera during that time.

Normally, this would just give you a blurry image. But in the dark, it will record a moving light as a line or mark, like a brush stroke. Keeping the light source in one place or moving it slowly will result in a stronger glow, while moving it faster will make a fainter line.

GARDEN GNOMON

Build your own ancient shadow clock in a garden or on the beach.

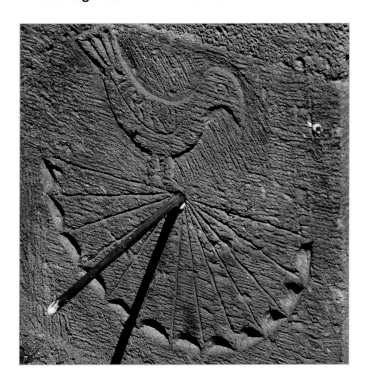

ANAXIMANDER

(c. 610–546 BCE)

Anaximander was an ancient Greek philosopher and scientist. He experimented with many things, including the **gnomon**, a stick stuck into the ground to cast a shadow. You can use a gnomon as a kind of clock, and also to map the seasons and **solstices**.

Anaximander didn't invent the gnomon—they existed long before his time, in places such as ancient Sumeria and ancient China. But he did design and build his own gnomons, and introduced them to ancient Greece.

WHAT YOU NEED

- a strong, straight stick at least 3.5 feet (1 m) long
- a sunny spot in a yard where your gnomon won't be disturbed
- 12 stones
- a bucket of soil or mulch (optional)
- a clock or watch
- a marker

If you don't have a yard to use, you might be able to make a gnomon in a school playground or on the beach (see right). This project will work best in summer, and if you are not close to the equator.

Step 1

Ask an adult to make a hole in the ground and push the stick into it. If this isn't possible, you can stand the stick in a bucket and fill it with mulch or soil to hold the stick upright.

Step 2

Wait until your clock or watch shows a time on the hour, such as 6 a.m. Put a stone on the shadow of the gnomon, and write the number 6 on the stone with a marker.

Step 3

Check the gnomon every hour, and add a stone to show where the shadow is for each hour, making a curved line of stones. It may take a few days to do this if it isn't always sunny.

Step 4

You can now use your gnomon as a clock, looking at where the shadow falls to see what time it is.

THE BEACH VERSION

Though the sea may wash it away, a gnomon is also a fun project for a day out at the beach. You can make the numbers with stones or shells.

SHADOW CLOCKS

A gnomon is one of the simplest and oldest clocks. It works because Earth rotates once a day, making the sun appear in different positions in the sky. This means that shadows fall in different places at different times.

However, a simple gnomon isn't very accurate because as summer becomes winter, the sun moves across a smaller part of the sky, and the shadows won't be in quite the same places. After Anaximander, other scientists improved the gnomon by making the stick lean over at an angle that matches the **axis** of Earth. The sundials you might see in gardens are usually at an angle. This makes the shadows for each hour fall in the same places, at every time of year.

LIGHT BOX DISPLAY

Make your own light box to display a moveable message or a work of art.

Many of Jeff Wall's artworks are photographs of carefully set up scenes, either remembered from real life, or recreated from paintings.

Jeff Wall, A Sudden Gust of Wind (after Hokusai)

JEFF WALL

(1946–)

Early in his career, Canadian photography artist Jeff Wall was inspired by the way large advertising billboards were often lit from behind, drawing attention to the glowing images. He decided to display some of his pictures in the same way, mounting them on huge light boxes, and these are now his most famous works.

A light box is a wide, shallow box with a translucent surface, lit from inside. Artists and designers often use them to see detail and color clearly. They have also become a popular room decoration, and come with letters or pictures that you can arrange on the front.

WHAT YOU NEED

- a shallow, sturdy cardboard box with a separate lid, such as a chocolate box
- a set of small battery-powered lights
- two clear plastic craft sheets
- invisible tape

- tracing paper
- pencil
- ruler
- scissors or craft knife
- markers, or a computer and printer

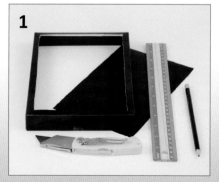

1

Step 1
Using the pencil and ruler, lightly draw a frame on the front of the box, about 0.5 inches (1 cm) in from the edge. Ask an adult to use scissors or a craft knife to cut out the middle as neatly as possible.

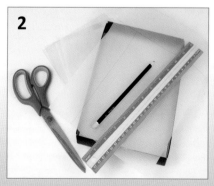

2

Step 2
Turn the lid over and measure the dimensions inside it. Measure out and cut two clear plastic craft sheets and four pieces of tracing paper the same size, so that they will fit neatly inside.

24

3

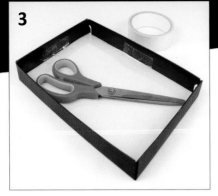

Step 3

Put one of the clear plastic sheets into the lid, then both pieces of tracing paper, then the other clear plastic sheet. Press them all down and use tape to stick them firmly to the inside of the lid.

4

Step 4

Put the lid aside. Use the scissors to cut a slot about 0.5 inches (1 cm) wide in the box itself, low down on one side. Put the lights into the box, with the wire leading out though the slot, so that the battery pack and switch are outside the box.

5

Step 5

Press the lights gently down into the box and secure them to the base by sticking down the cable between each light with pieces of tape. Put the lid on and switch on the lights to see your light box lit up.

6

Step 6

To display a photograph or artwork on your light box, you can either draw a picture directly onto a piece of tracing paper, or print out a photograph or artwork onto tracing paper. Trim it to the right size and tape it to the front of the light box to display it.

7&8

Step 7

To make a message light box, cut two strips of clear plastic craft sheet, the same length as the box and about 0.5 inches (1 cm) wide. Use invisible tape to attach them to the front edges of the light box to create letter slots.

Step 8

Use a computer to write large alphabet letters in an interesting font, and print them out onto tracing paper. Cut the printout into small rectangles, each with one letter on it. Slip the letters underneath the strips of clear plastic to spell a message.

ATTRACTED TO LIGHT

We know that moths are drawn towards light, but scientists have found that humans are too. Studies have found that people will choose to sit facing a wall that is lit up, and they will pay more attention to light that is moving or flashing, or contrasts strongly with a darker background. This is why light boxes, neon signs, and flashing messages are effective ways of advertising.

DIFFUSE LIGHT!

A light box wouldn't work as well if there were lights behind clear glass or plastic sheet. Instead, the light needs to be **diffused**, or spread out evenly, to make a gently glowing backdrop that doesn't interfere with the image. Your light box uses tracing paper to get this effect, as it's **translucent**, meaning it's not completely see-through but is clear enough to let some light through. A professional light box uses translucent glass or plastic.

NEON SIGN

Make your own neon sign to share a message with the world!

TRACEY EMIN

(1963–)

Tracey Emin is a leading British artist who makes many different kinds of works, including paintings, drawings, sculptures, and art installations. She often uses words and messages in her art, such as **neon** signs. They combine eye-catching glowing color with the thought and emotion of words. Emin's signs are made of glass and use neon gas, like the signs used on stores and movie theaters. Since these neon signs would be very difficult to make at home, you can use a type of wire that lights up, called **electroluminescent** (EL) wire, to make your own realistic-looking neon sign.

> "Being an artist isn't just about making nice things, or people patting you on the back; it's some kind of communication, a message."
>
> *– Tracey Emin*

Tracey Emin's neon sign artwork Trust Yourself, *2014.*

WHAT YOU NEED

- a pencil and paper
- a length of ready-to-use EL wire, about 6.5 to 10 feet (2 to 3 m) long and about 0.8 inches (2–3 mm) thick, with a battery pack attached (see panel below)
- batteries to fit the battery pack
- bendable garden wire (the same length as the EL wire)
- pliers
- wire cutters (these are often part of the pliers)
- clear or invisible tape

Step 1

Decide on what you want to write. 6.5 to 10 feet (2 to 3 m) of wire should be enough for one word or a short two-word phrase. Sketch out how you would like it to look, remembering that all the letters will have to be connected.

EL wire is often sold as a ready-to-use kit with a battery pack and switch already included. It comes in many different colors and widths, and some have flashing options too. You can find it in hobby and electronics stores, or online (see page 31). Before making your sign, insert the batteries and check your wire works.

Step 2

With an adult's help, cut off a piece of garden wire the same length as your EL wire. Use the pliers to bend over the sharp ends and squeeze them in tightly so they don't scratch you while you're working.

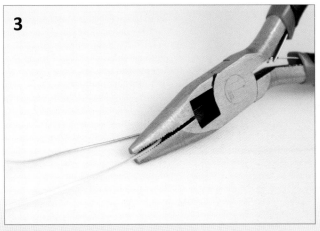

Step 3

Now start to gently bend and shape the garden wire to make your word. It can be tricky, so ask an adult to help if necessary. To make sharp corners, hold the wire tightly in the pliers and bend it close to where the pliers are holding it.

Step 4

When your word is finished, press it against a hard surface to make it as flat as possible. Cut off any excess garden wire, and fold the cut end over again so that it's not sharp.

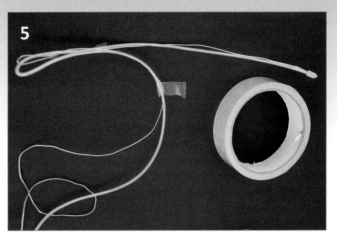

Step 5

Now you can attach the EL wire. Start at the loose end of the wire, not the battery end. Carefully line up the EL wire with the garden wire, bit by bit, and attach them together using small pieces of tape. Once the sign is lit up, they will be almost invisible.

Step 6

As you work, make sure you are keeping the EL wire on top of the garden wire all the way along. Where the garden wire ends and the EL wire extends and leads to the battery pack, use extra tape to make it extra strong.

WHAT TO WRITE

Stuck for ideas? How about…

- Your favorite band, song, or sport
- A pet's name
- A message to the world, like "Be happy!"

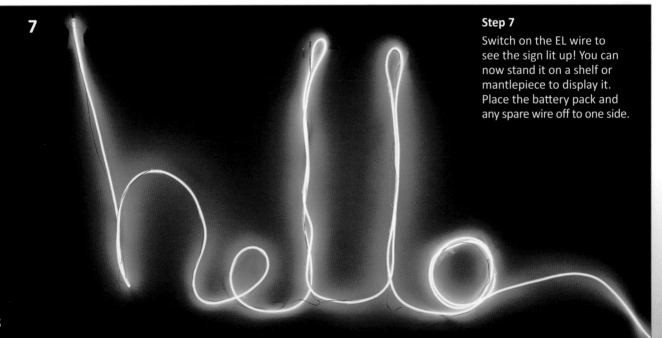

Step 7

Switch on the EL wire to see the sign lit up! You can now stand it on a shelf or mantlepiece to display it. Place the battery pack and any spare wire off to one side.

Buildings in big cities are often illuminated with neon lights.

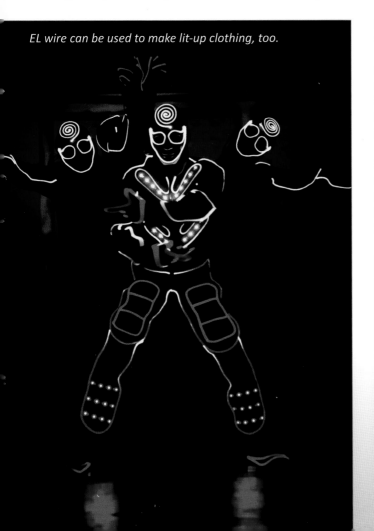

EL wire can be used to make lit-up clothing, too.

LIGHT IN A TUBE

A real neon light is made using a glass tube with **electrodes** at the ends, attached to an electric circuit. Neon gas, or another gas, such as **argon** or **xenon**, is sealed inside the tube. When it's switched on, the flow of electricity makes the gas glow.

EL wire works in a different way. It contains a copper wire coated with a chemical that glows when an **electric current** passes through it. It's covered in colored plastic tubing to give the wire its color. As EL wire is flexible, it's easy to make into any shape you like.

LIGHT YOURSELF UP

Lit-up jackets or t-shirts are great for parties and for festivals where it can be hard to find your friends and family in the dark. To make one, use a needle and thread to sew a length of EL wire to your garment in a pattern or shape. Position it so that some of the wire is spare at the end, and you can put the battery pack into a pocket.

GLOSSARY

animalcules A name invented by Antonie van Leeuwenhoek for the tiny creatures he saw using his microscope

argon A type of gas used to make colored electric tube lights

artificial Made by humans, such as a light bulb, rather than naturally occurring, such as sunlight

axis The imaginary line between the North and South Poles that Earth spins around

bacteria A type of tiny living thing that can be seen using a microscope

camera obscura A dark box or room used to capture an image of the world outside it

diffuse Spread out evenly

electric current A flow of electricity

electrode A part of an electric circuit that makes makes contact with a non-metallic substance, such as air

electroluminescent A type of wire that glows when an electric current flows through it

fiber optics Thin and clear fibers of plastic or glass that carry light through an enclosed material

fiber optic cable Cable containing fine flexible glass tubes that light can travel along

gnomon The raised part of a sundial that casts a shadow

internal reflection The way light bounces off the inside of a fiber-optic cable or tube

lens A curved, clear object used to make light bend, or refract, as it passes through it

light rays The straight paths that light waves follow as they travel forwards

microbes Very small living things that can only be seen with a microscope

microwaves A type of invisible light wave with a long wavelength

neon A type of gas used to make colored electric tube lights

periscope A tube with mirrors and lenses and through which an observer can see around corners or above walls

radio waves A type of invisible light wave with a very long wavelength

reflection The way light bounces off surfaces, especially light or shiny surfaces such as a mirror

refraction The way light can change direction as it passes from one clear material into another

retina The layer of light-sensitive cells inside the back of the eye

solar power Energy from the sun that is collected and used to generate electricity or power machines

solstice The summer solstice is the day of the year with the most hours of daylight, and the winter solstice is the day of the year with the fewest hours of daylight

translucent Not completely see-through but clear enough to let some light through so that objects are not clearly visible

visible light The range of wavelengths of light that the human eye can detect

wavelength The length of a light wave, or other wave, measured from the top of one wave to the top of the next

xenon A type of gas used to make colored electric tube lights

x-rays A type of invisible light wave with a short wavelength

FURTHER INFORMATION

WEBSITES ABOUT LIGHT

Science Kids: Light
www.sciencekids.co.nz/light.html

Optics for Kids
http://optics.synopsys.com/
learn/kids/optics-kids-light.html

Optics4Kids
www.optics4kids.org/home

Climate Kids NASA: Light Bulbs
www.climatekids.nasa.gov/light-bulbs

WEBSITES ABOUT MAKING

Exploratorium: After Image
www.exploratorium.edu/snacks

Exploratorium: Colored Shadows
www.exploratorium.edu/snacks/
colored-shadows

Instructables: Batman Light
www.instructables.com/id/Batman-Light

Maker Camp: LED Magnetic Dart Board
https://makercamp.com/projects/
led-magnetic-dartboard

WHERE TO BUY MATERIALS

Electronics stores
For electronic components and making projects

Michaels
For art and craft materials
www.michaels.com

The Home Depot
For pipes, tubing, wood, glue, and other hardware
www.homedepot.com

BOOKS

Bright, Michael. *From Sunshine to Light Bulb*.
Crabtree, 2017.

Johnson, Robin. *The Science of Light Waves*.
Crabtree, 2017.

Kenney, Karen Latchana. *The Science of Color:
Investigating Light*. Abdo, 2016.

Shaffer, Jody Jensen. *Vampires and Light*.
Capstone Press, 2013.

Spilsbury, Richard. *Investigating Electricity*. Crabtree, 2018.

Spilsbury, Richard. *Investigating Light*. Crabtree, 2018.

PLACES TO VISIT

California Science Center, Los Angeles, California
www.californiasciencecenter.org

New York Hall of Science, Corona New York
www.nysci.org/visit

Ontario Science Centre, Toronto, Ontario
www.ontariosciencecentre.ca

Michigan Science Center
www.mi-sci.org

INDEX